IN THE
NIGHT SKY

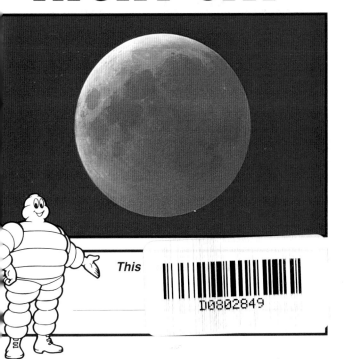

This

D0802849

LEARNING ABOUT STARS

A good way of learning about the stars is to visit a **planetarium**, where a special projector shows the night sky on the inside of a dome. At least there it is warm, so you can learn the sky in comfort!

Another good way of finding out which stars can be seen, and at what times, is to use a

planisphere. This is a special map of the sky, marked so that you can set it for any date and time. It then shows exactly what you will be able to see.

I-Spy for **10**:
a **planetarium**.
Double when you visit one

I-Spy for **10**:
a **planisphere**.
Double if you have one

With the naked eye you can see about 8500 stars over the whole sky.

3

You don't have to have a telescope to look at the night sky. You can see lots of things with just your eyes. If you can, borrow a pair of binoculars. They are often much better even than big telescopes in helping you to see things in the sky.

a refractor

Amateur astronomers use various types of telescopes. One, known as a **refractor**, uses lenses at each end of a tube. You look straight through it at the sky. Another type, known as a **reflector**, uses mirrors instead of lenses and you have to look in the side of the tube.

Some telescopes use both lenses and mirrors. They are popular with amateur astronomers because they are easy to carry from place to place. The type you may see is called a **Schmidt-Cassegrain**, named after two astronomers who designed telescopes.

I-Spy for **10**: a **refractor**. Double for one mounted on a stand so that it can turn to any part of the sky.

I-Spy for **10**: a **reflector**. Double if you know how many mirrors it has inside it.

I-Spy for **10**: a **Schmidt-Cassegrain** telescope

⬆ *a reflector* ⬇ *a Schmidt-Cassegrain*

I-Spy through a telescope for **10**. Double if you can say what is unexpected about what you see!

With binoculars you can see about 50 000 stars over the whole sky.

Although the stars are actually scattered about in space, they look as if they are on the inside of a giant dome. When you stand outside — like the little figure in the diagram — the stars are overhead and the horizon is all around you.

Just as the Sun moves across the sky in the day, so the stars move during the night, because the Earth itself is rotating. One star, called **Polaris**, appears to stand still at the North Pole of the sky, and all the other stars seem to rotate around it. Only in a photograph, such as the one shown here, can you see that Polaris is not quite at the North Pole. The exposure needed for the

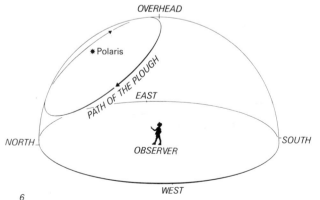

OVERHEAD

* Polaris

PATH OF THE PLOUGH

EAST

NORTH

OBSERVER

SOUTH

WEST

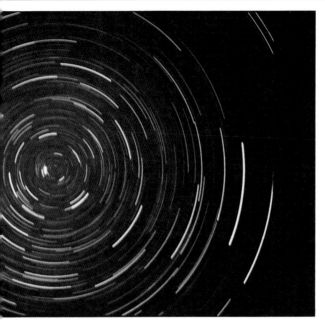

photograph was several hours, and all the stars have left trails as the sky moved. The very short, bright trail near the centre was made by Polaris.

The circle in the diagram shows the path around Polaris that is followed by the group of stars called the **Plough**. They never dip below the horizon because they are very close to the North Pole. Because the Earth revolves around the Sun once a year, the Sun appears to move slowly across the sky, hiding different stars during the daytime as the months go by. So the stars that you see at night also change with the time of year. Later in this book you can see what the sky looks like at four different seasons.

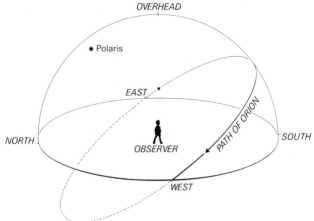

To help them find their way around the sky, ancient peoples invented names for various groups of stars, or **constellations**. Astronomers use the Latin names for constellations, so everyone, anywhere on Earth, knows which groups of stars they are talking about. Most bright stars have individual names, and these often come from Arabic words that described their positions in the imaginary constellation patterns on the sky.

Many constellations are farther away from Polaris and the North Pole than the Plough, so they rise and set during the night. The diagram shows how a constellation called **Orion** rises above the horizon in the east, becomes highest in the south, and then disappears as it sets in the west.

*I-Spy for **10**: a book with old drawings of **constellations**. Double if you know how many constellations cover the whole sky. Score **10** if you know the English name for **Orion***

The Planets

Stars shine because they are extremely hot and give

out their own light. The Moon and **planets**, on the other hand, only reflect light from the Sun. Two planets, **Venus** and **Jupiter**, shine like very bright stars, and two others, **Mars** and **Saturn**, although fainter, are also sometimes easy to see. All these planets (and the other, fainter ones) orbit the Sun like the Earth.

The planets do not have fixed positions like the stars, so they cannot be drawn on the maps here. You can sometimes find details of where they are in the newspapers. Venus is always close to the Sun, so it is in the west in the evening, and in the east early in the morning.

I-Spy for 10:
Venus *in the evening. Double in the morning.*

I-Spy for 10:
Jupiter*. Double if you know how many planets there are.*

I-Spy for 20:
Mars *(which is red)*

I-Spy for 20:
Saturn

planets over London

9

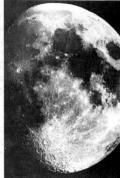

crescent   *waxing gibbous*   *waning gibbous*

As the Moon goes around the Earth, we see it by the light from the Sun that it reflects. It always turns the same side towards us, so sometimes it is in darkness, sometimes partly lit, and sometimes a complete, bright circle.

When the Moon appears as a very thin **crescent** in the western sky shortly after sunset, it is called **New Moon**. The ends of the crescent (the **horns**) are turned towards the east. As the days go

Full Moon

waning crescent

by, the Moon appears farther towards the east at sunset, and the bright area waxes (increases). When half the Moon can be seen, it is called **First Quarter**. The bright area continues to increase, until the whole face of the Moon is shining at **Full Moon**. The Moon then begins to wane (decrease), first through **Last Quarter**, then to the **waning crescent**, until it disappears close to the Sun in the east at sunrise. Between First Quarter and Full, and between Full and Last Quarter, the Moon is called **gibbous**.

Sometimes when the Moon is a crescent, you can see the rest of the Moon faintly illuminated by sunlight that has been reflected from the Earth on to the dark part of the Moon. This is called **Earthshine**.

Some parts of the Moon's surface are darker than others. These dark grey areas are called **maria**. They are flat lava plains. The lighter areas are called the **highlands**, and they contain nearly all the craters that pock-mark the face of the Moon.

I-Spy for **10**: the **crescent** Moon ☐

I-Spy for **10**: the **horns** of the crescent ☐

I-Spy for **10**: **New Moon** ☐

I-Spy for **10**: **First Quarter** ☐

I-Spy for **10**: **Full Moon** ☐

I-Spy for **10**: **Last Quarter** ☐

I-Spy for **20**: the **waning crescent** ☐

I-Spy for **10**: the **gibbous** Moon ☐

I-Spy for **10**: **Earthshine** ☐

I-Spy for **10**: the **maria**. Double for the meaning of the name ☐

I-Spy for **10**: the **highlands** ☐

a meteor

As you watch the sky, especially at dawn and dusk, you will often see a slow-moving point of light crossing the sky. This is an artificial **satellite**, orbiting the Earth.

Sometimes you see a sudden, short streak of light. This is often called a 'shooting star', but its proper name is a **meteor**. (They are not stars, but are tiny grains of dust that are burnt up as they dash through the Earth's atmosphere.) On a few nights of the year, the Earth passes through a cloud of dust, and we have a **meteor shower**, with

a meteorite

12

a comet

dozens of meteors each hour. Very rarely indeed, a meteor is brighter than any of the stars or planets; then it is called a **fireball**.

Occasionally, some meteors are large enough to land on Earth. You can see these **meteorites** in many different museums.

You may be lucky enough to see a **comet**. Only rarely do these become bright enough for you to see them with the naked eye. A comet is a mixture of ice and dust — meteor dust comes from comets — and the heat from the Sun often makes it grow a long tail.

I-Spy for **10**: a **satellite**

I-Spy for **10**: a **meteor**

I-Spy for **30**: a **meteor shower**

I-Spy for **50**: a **fireball**

I-Spy for **50**: a **comet**

Halley's Comet is the most famous. It returns every seventy-six years, most recently in 1986.

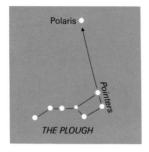

THE PLOUGH

In the northern part of the sky you will find the **Plough** (or **Dipper** in North America), a group of seven bright stars with an easily remembered shape, rather like a saucepan with a long handle. It forms just part of the constellation of **Ursa Major**, the Great Bear. The picture shows how the constellation used to be drawn on old maps of the sky. The two end stars of the Plough are called the **Pointers**, because a line through them points to **Polaris** (page 6), the star that stands still. The Pointers are called **Dubhe** and **Merak**.

Polaris is the brightest star in **Ursa Minor**, the Little Bear (*see* page 16). The two stars closest to Ursa Major are known as **The Guards**, and one, **Kochab**, is quite bright. The diagram opposite shows how the two constellations appear to swing round the North Pole (and Polaris) during the course of the night.

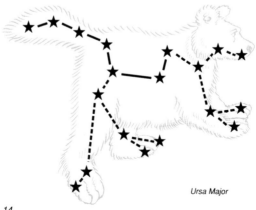

Ursa Major

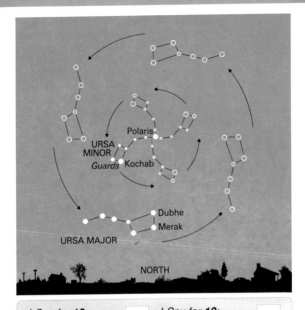

I-Spy for **10**: the **Plough**	☐	I-Spy for **10**: **Ursa Minor**	☐
I-Spy for **10**: **Dubhe**	☐	I-Spy for **10**: **Kochab**	☐
I-Spy for **10**: **Merak**	☐	I-Spy for **10**: **The Guards**	☐
I-Spy for **10**: **Polaris**. Double if you know another name for it.	☐	Score **10** if you know why the Great and Little Bears appear odd in all old constellation drawings	☐
I-Spy for **10**: the other stars in **Ursa Major**	☐		

There are several other constellations near the North Pole. If you find the star called **Megrez**, where Ursa Major's 'tail' joins the body, and imagine a line from there to Polaris and beyond, you come to a group of five stars in the shape of a 'W' — or an 'M' when they are the other way up! These form the constellation of **Cassiopeia**, an ancient, legendary queen.

Snaking its way around the Pole is a long, faint constellation called **Draco**, the Dragon. At the end of its long, winding 'body' four stars make up its lozenge-shaped 'head'. The star between Mizar (in Ursa Major) and the Guards is called **Thuban**.

Between the head of Draco and Cassiopeia is the constellation of **Cepheus**, a legendary king, husband of Cassiopeia. The stars in this constellation form a pointed shape like the gable end of a house.

I-Spy for **10**:
Megrez

I-Spy for **10**:
Cassiopeia

I-Spy for **10**:
Draco

I-Spy for **10**:
Mizar.
Double if you can say what is strange about it. (Look at it through binoculars if you are not quite sure.)

I-Spy for **10**:
Thuban

I-Spy for **10**:
Cepheus

Ursa Minor

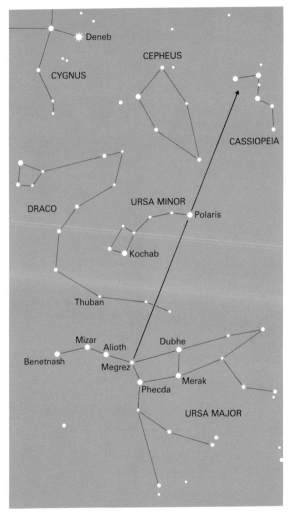

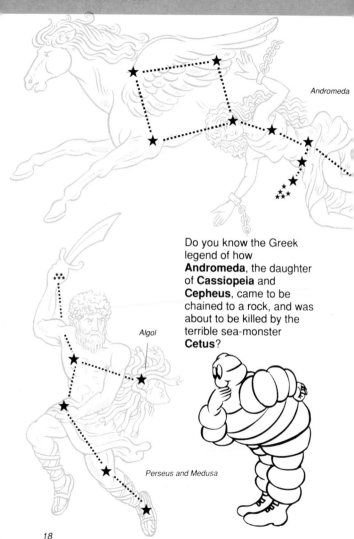

Andromeda

Do you know the Greek legend of how **Andromeda**, the daughter of **Cassiopeia** and **Cepheus**, came to be chained to a rock, and was about to be killed by the terrible sea-monster **Cetus**?

Algol

Perseus and Medusa

She was rescued just in time by **Perseus**, who had earlier killed the dreadful Gorgon, Medusa. Medusa's head, with snakes for hair, turned anyone who looked at it to stone. (Perseus was clever and looked in a mirror.) He showed the head to Cetus, who became a rock.

You can find all these legendary beings in the sky (*see* the maps on pages 28 and 38, for example). The old constellation drawing of Perseus shows him holding Medusa's head. This is represented in the sky by the star **Algol**, whose name comes from the Arabic words *Al Guhl*, meaning 'the demon'.

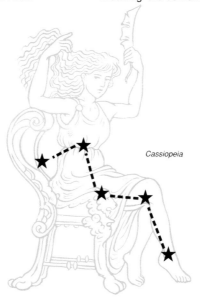

Cassiopeia

I-Spy for **10**: **Perseus**		I-Spy for **10**: **Algol**	

Cygnus

from Cygnus down towards the stars of **Sagittarius** (page 35). **Albireo** is the 'beak' of the Swan, which appears to be flying down the Milky Way. Can you see the **Great Dark Rift** in Cygnus? (*See* the drawing on the next page.) This may look like a 'hole in the stars', but actually there are just as many as elsewhere in the Milky Way, but most are hidden by dark clouds of dust between the stars.

High in the sky in the middle of summer is the **Summer Triangle**, the corners of which are formed by the very bright stars **Deneb** in **Cygnus**, the Swan, **Vega** in **Lyra**, the Lyre, and **Altair** in **Aquila**, the Eagle.

The **Milky Way** is a silvery band of light that stretches right across the sky and is easiest to see in this part of the sky. The faint light comes from hundreds of thousands of stars which are so closely crowded together that you cannot see them as individual stars. With binoculars you can see that there appears no limit to the number of stars in the Milky Way.

The densest part of the northern Milky Way runs

*I-Spy for **10**:*
Cygnus

*I-Spy for **10**:*
Deneb

*I-Spy for **10**:*
Lyra

*I-Spy for **10**:*
Vega

*I-Spy for **10**:*
Aquila

*I-Spy for **10**:*
Altair

*I-Spy for **10**:*
the **Milky Way**

*I-Spy for **10**:*
Albireo

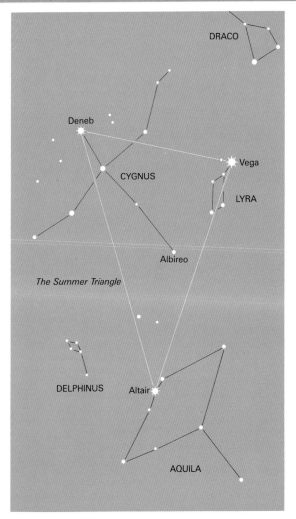

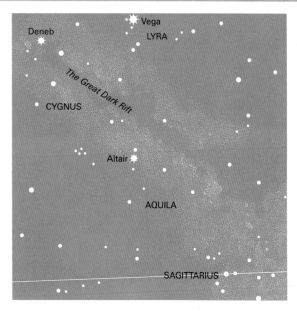

The Sun and our Solar System lie inside a huge flattened system of stars, the **Galaxy**. As we look out, we see the disc edge-on, stretching right around the sky as the Milky Way. There are about a hundred thousand million stars in our Galaxy, and most are too far away to be seen properly with even the largest telescope.

Inside our own Galaxy, stars are born in groups (known as **clusters**) from the material between the stars. Those with young, blue stars are known as **open clusters**, and usually contain a few tens of stars, which are only a few million years old. The most famous open cluster is the **Pleiades**, in Taurus (*see* map page 28). But there are other clusters that are much older — probably ten thousand million years. These globular clusters are spherical in shape and

s ↓ globular cluster M13

each contains many thousands of stars. The most famous is **M13**, in Hercules (*see* map page 40).

I-Spy for **10**: the **Pleiades**

I-Spy for **10**: **M13** in Hercules

Score **10** if you know the size of the largest telescope on Earth

This chart shows all the stars that you can see if you live in the Northern Hemisphere. With it you can find your way from one constellation to another. The North Pole of the sky and **Polaris** are in the centre.

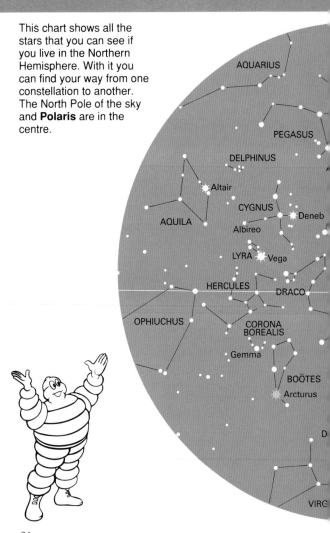

AQUARIUS

PEGASUS

DELPHINUS

Altair

CYGNUS

Deneb

AQUILA

Albireo

LYRA   Vega

HERCULES

DRACO

OPHIUCHUS

CORONA
BOREALIS

Gemma

BOÖTES

Arcturus

D

VIRG

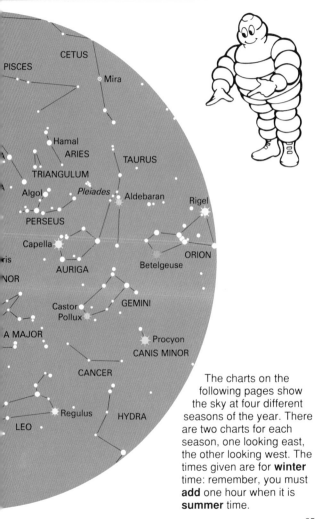

CETUS

PISCES

Mira

Hamal
ARIES
TRIANGULUM
TAURUS

Algol   *Pleiades*   Aldebaran   Rigel
PERSEUS

Capella
ORION
AURIGA   Betelgeuse

Castor   GEMINI
Pollux

A MAJOR

Procyon
CANIS MINOR

CANCER

Regulus   HYDRA
LEO

The charts on the
following pages show
the sky at four different
seasons of the year. There
are two charts for each
season, one looking east,
the other looking west. The
times given are for **winter**
time: remember, you must
add one hour when it is
summer time.

25

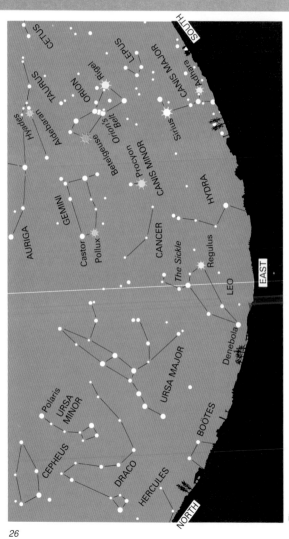

Times:

Late December	Late January	Late February	
Early January	Early February	Early March	
11 pm	9 pm		7 pm
10 pm	8 pm		6 pm

Now is the best time to see **Orion** and the stars of **Canis Major** and **Canis Minor,** the Greater and Lesser Dogs. **Betelgeuse,** in Orion, is a gigantic type of star, called a red supergiant. If it were in the Solar System in place of the Sun, the Earth would lie below its surface. Its colour is in sharp contrast to bluish-white **Rigel** on the other side of the constellation. **Sirius,** in Canis Major, is the brightest star in the sky. Venus and Jupiter, which are planets (page 9), are the only objects that ever appear brighter than it does.

I-Spy for **10**:
Orion

I-Spy for **10**:
the stars of Orion's Belt

I-Spy for **10**:
red Betelgeuse

I-Spy for **10**:
blue-white Rigel

I-Spy for **10**:
Canis Major

I-Spy for **10**:
Sirius. Double if you know another name for it.

I-Spy for **10**:
Adhara

Orion

27

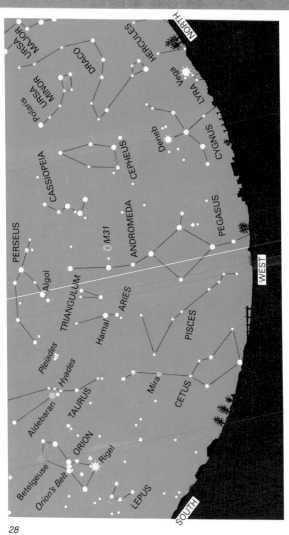

Times:
Late December   11 pm   Late January   9 pm   Late February   7 pm
Early January   10 pm   Early February   8 pm   Early March   6 pm

28

Altair, one of the stars of the Summer Triangle (page 20) has disappeared, but Vega can still be seen low on the horizon in the north-west, while **Deneb** is higher up in the same part of the sky. Andromeda, with its great galaxy (page 39) and the small neighbouring constellations of **Triangulum**, the Triangle, and **Aries**, the Ram, with one bright star, **Hamal**, are still easy to see.

High in the south is the constellation of **Perseus**, and lower down, **Taurus**, the Bull, whose 'eye' is orange **Aldebaran**. Taurus contains two clusters, the Pleiades (page 22) and the 'V' of stars near Aldebaran, known as the **Hyades.**

I-Spy for 10:
Taurus

I-Spy for 10:
Aldebaran

I-Spy for 10:
the Hyades cluster

I-Spy for 10:
Triangulum

I-Spy for 10:
Aries

I-Spy for 10:
Hamal

Cepheus

29

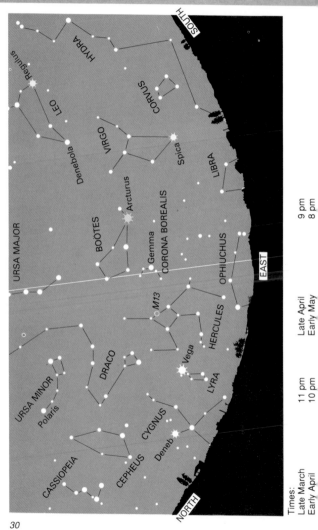

Times:

| Late March | 11 pm | Late April | 9 pm |
| Early April | 10 pm | Early May | 8 pm |

If you follow the line of the Pointers, but in the opposite direction, you come to the great constellation of **Leo**, the Lion. The 'backward question mark' of stars (with **Regulus** as the 'dot') forming the lion's head (*see the next chart page 32*) is known as **The Sickle**.

At the other end of Leo, **Denebola** forms the 'tail' of the lion. You can follow the curve of the tail of Ursa Major, or a line from Regulus to Denebola, to help you find **Arcturus**, the brightest star in **Boötes**, the Herdsman. Low on the horizon are the four stars of **Corvus**, the Crow.

see the next chart page 32

I-Spy for **10**:
Pointers

I-Spy for **10**:
Leo

I-Spy for **10**:
Regulus

I-Spy for **10**:
The Sickle

I-Spy for **10**:
Denebola

I-Spy for **10**:
orange **Arcturus**

I-Spy for **10**:
Boötes

I-Spy for **10**:
Corvus

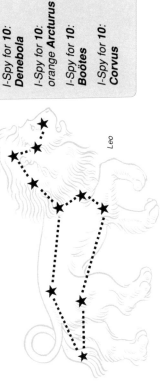

Leo

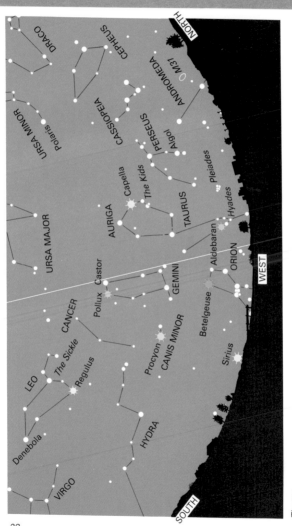

Times:

| Late March | 11 pm | Late April | 9 pm |
| Early April | 10 pm | Early May | 8 pm |

32

Now is a good time to see the constellation of **Gemini**, the Twins, which consists of two, almost parallel lines of stars, running west from the two bright stars **Castor** and **Pollux**. Between Leo and Gemini is the faint constellation of **Cancer**, the Crab. Below Gemini is the small constellation of **Canis Minor**, the Lesser Dog, with just one bright star, **Procyon**. High in the north-west is the constellation of **Auriga**, the Charioteer. In old drawings he is shown carrying two young goats in his arms, so the little triangle of stars to the right of **Capella** is known as **The Kids**.

I-Spy for 10:
Gemini

I-Spy for 10:
Castor

I-Spy for 10:
Pollux

I-Spy for 10:
Cancer

I-Spy for 10:
Canis Minor

I-Spy for 10:
Procyon

I-Spy for 10:
Auriga

I-Spy for 10:
Capella

I-Spy for 10:
The Kids

Taurus

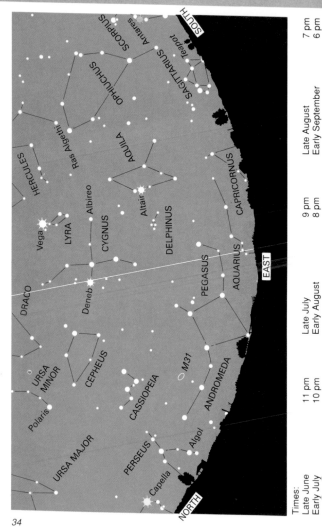

Times:
Late June / Early July — 11 pm / 10 pm
Late July / Early August — 11 pm / 10 pm
Late August / Early September — 9 pm / 8 pm
7 pm / 6 pm

Although it does not get dark until very late and the nights are short, now is the best time to see the great **Summer Triangle** (page 20) and the star clouds of the **Milky Way**, which consist of thousands and thousands of stars, too close together to be seen as separate points of light.

Very low in the south is **Sagittarius**, the Archer. Can you spy the 'Teapot' among its stars? To the east is the fainter constellation of **Capricornus**, the Sea-Goat, and the rather brighter one of **Aquarius**, the Water Carrier. Between them and Cygnus lies the tiny constellation of **Delphinus**, the Dolphin.

☐ *I-Spy for 10:* the **Summer Triangle**

☐ *I-Spy for 10:* **Sagittarius**

☐ *I-Spy for 10:* the **'Teapot'**

☐ *I-Spy for 10:* **Capricornus**

☐ *I-Spy for 10:* **Aquarius**

☐ *I-Spy for 10:* **Delphinus**

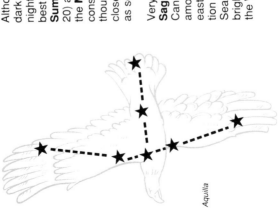

Aquilla

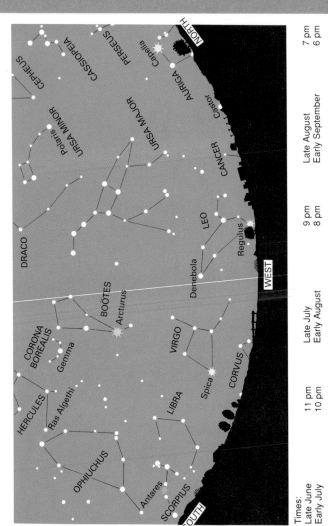

Times: Late June / Early July — SOUTH

11 pm / 10 pm — Late July / Early August

9 pm / 8 pm — Late August / Early September

7 pm / 6 pm

WEST

NORTH

SOUTH

36

I-Spy for 10:
Spica

I-Spy for 10:
Virgo

I-Spy for 10:
Corona Borealis

I-Spy for 10:
Gemma

I-Spy for 10:
Ophiuchus

I-Spy for 10:
Scorpius

I-Spy for 10:
red **Antares**

I-Spy for 10:
Libra

If you follow the curve of the tail of the Plough (as described on page 31) and go beyond Arcturus, you come to **Spica**, the brightest star in the constellation of **Virgo**, the Virgin. East of Boötes is the semi-circle of stars of the constellation of **Corona Borealis**, the Northern Crown. The brightest star is called **Gemma**, the Jewel.

To the east lies the large constellation of **Ophiuchus**, the Serpent Bearer. Below this is **Scorpius**, the Scorpion. Its brightest star is **Antares**, the 'Rival of Mars', so called because, like the planet, it is deep red in colour. Between Antares and Spica, lies the constellation of **Libra**, the Balance (or Scales).

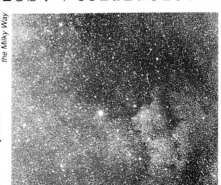

the Milky Way

37

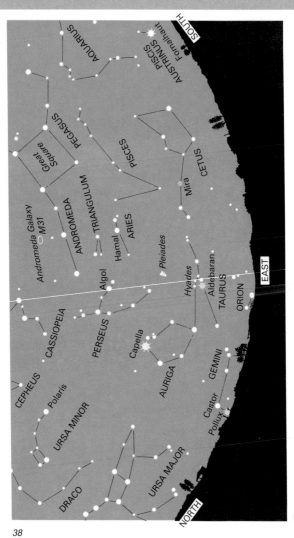

38

I-Spy for 10:
Pegasus

I-Spy for 10:
Andromeda

I-Spy for 30:
*the Great
Andromeda Galaxy*

I-Spy for 10:
Pisces

I-Spy for 10:
Cetus

I-Spy for 20:
Fomalhaut

Rising high in the east is the **Great Square of Pegasus**. The star at the north-eastern corner actually belongs to **Andromeda**. Part of the way along the line of four bright stars in Andromeda, two more point at right-angles to the north, indicating the position of the **Great Andromeda Galaxy** (also known as **M31**). It needs to be very clear and dark for you to see this galaxy. Just think, the light you see started its journey at about the time when the first humans began to evolve from ape-like creatures!

Below Pegasus lies the faint constellation of **Pisces**, the Fishes, and still farther south, there is the large area of sky known as **Cetus**, the Sea Monster. Unfortunately many of the stars in this area are rather faint. If you are lucky, however, you may just be able to see, very very low in the south, **Fomalhaut** in Piscis Austrinus, the Southern Fish.

the Great Andromeda Galaxy

39

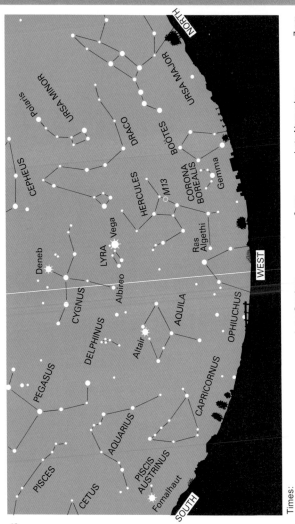

NORTH

WEST

SOUTH

7 pm
6 pm

Late November
Early December

9 pm
8 pm

Late October
Early November

11 pm
10 pm

Times:
Late September
Early October

URSA MAJOR

URSA MINOR

Polaris

DRACO

BOÖTES

CEPHEUS

HERCULES

M13

CORONA
BOREALIS

Gemma

Vega

LYRA

Ras
Algethi

Deneb

Albireo

CYGNUS

AQUILA

OPHIUCHUS

DELPHINUS

Altair

PEGASUS

CAPRICORNUS

AQUARIUS

PISCIS
AUSTRINUS

PISCES

CETUS

Fomalhaut

40

Altair (see page 20) as well as much of the **Milky Way** which also runs through the constellations of **Cassiopeia** and **Perseus**.

Like the constellations of Andromeda and Pegasus, **Hercules**, the legendary hero, is upside down! One foot rests on Draco in the north. The name of one star **Ras Algethi**, means 'the kneeling man's head' in Arabic. The main part of his body is known as the 'Keystone' because the arrangement of the four stars is just like the shape of the central stone in an archway. On the western side of the Keystone lies the globular cluster, **M13** (see page 23).

It is still possible to see most of the **Summer Triangle** and the bright stars of **Vega**, **Deneb**, and

I-Spy for 10:
Hercules. *Double for the number of labours he had to accomplish.*

I-Spy for 10:
Ras Algethi

I-Spy for 20:
the cluster M13

Hercules

41

lunar eclipse

Sometimes the Earth comes between the Sun and the Moon and casts its shadow on the Moon. (It does not always do this, because the Moon is sometimes above and sometimes below the line connecting the Earth and the Sun.) This is a **lunar eclipse**, and only happens at Full Moon (page 11). The Earth's atmosphere lets some red light through, so the Moon appears **red**.

Sometimes the Moon comes between the Sun and the Earth (at New Moon). This is a **solar eclipse** where the Sun is hidden from view. But the Moon only throws a tiny shadow on the surface of the Earth, so you are much less likely to see one. You are more likely to see a **partial solar eclipse** when the Moon hides just part of the Sun.

(Remember, you must NEVER look at the Sun through binoculars or a telescope, because it would damage your eyes or even blind you.)

Quite frequently, the Sun sends out streams of charged (that is, electrified) particles. When these hit the Earth's atmosphere, they cause the air to glow, giving an **aurora** changing patterns of light high in the sky.

↑ *solar eclipse*　　　　　　　　↓ *aurora*

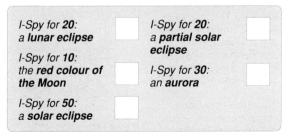

*I-Spy for **20**:* a **lunar eclipse**	☐	*I-Spy for **20**:* a **partial solar eclipse**	☐
*I-Spy for **10**:* the **red colour of the Moon**	☐	*I-Spy for **30**:* an **aurora**	☐
*I-Spy for **50**:* a **solar eclipse**	☐		

OBSERVATORIES

You may be lucky enough to visit an **observatory**. This is where professional astronomers study the stars. They often have several **telescopes**, which are usually very large reflectors (page 4). Do not expect to be able to look through one, though! The telescopes are only used with highly complicated cameras and other equipment.

A telescope is usually protected by a **dome** which has a slit that can open so that the telescope can look out. The domes themselves rotate to enable any part of the sky to be observed.

There are also observatories that use **radio telescopes**. These are often gigantic dishes that can pick up the faint radio signals coming from stars and galaxies thousands of millions of light-years away.

an observatory

a large professional telescope

I-Spy for **10**:
an **observatory**

I-Spy for **10**:
a **dome**

I-Spy for **10**:
a **great telescope**

I-Spy for **10**:
a **radio observatory**

I-Spy for **10**:
a **radio telescope**

Astronomers
measure distances
in light-years — the
number of years
it takes light to
travel from the
stars to us. Light
travels at nearly
300 000 kilometres
per second
(186 000 mps).

45

You can learn a lot about astronomy by visiting a museum. There you will often find displays explaining about planets, stars, galaxies, and other strange things like black holes! But you can also see many of the old instruments that earlier astronomers used.

One of the simplest devices is a **celestial sphere** which shows the stars, usually with the old constellation drawings. Another, much more complicated instrument is an **astrolabe** which is a special form of sky map. A planisphere (page 3) is a simplified modern version.

an astrolabe

You may also see an **armilliary sphere** which is a collection of rings that can be used to show the movements of the Sun, Moon and stars in the sky. Or you may find an **orrery** which is a working model of the Solar System where the planets move at correct relative speeds around the Sun.

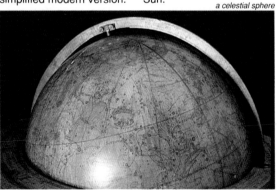

a celestial sphere

an orrery

I-Spy for **10**:
a **celestial sphere**.
Double for what is
odd about it.

I-Spy for **10**:
an **armilliary
sphere**

I-Spy for **10**:
an **astrolabe**

I-Spy for **10**:
an **orrery**

INDEX

Answers

Reflector telescope: 2 mirrors. Telescope: the image is upside-down. Constellations: 88. Orion: The Hunter. Jupiter (Planets): there are 9 planets. Mars: seas. Polaris: Pole Star. Great and Little Bears: the Bears have tails. Mizar: it is a double star. Largest telescope: either a 6-m telescope in the Caucasus, or a 10-m telescope under construction in Hawaii. Sirius: Dog Star. Hercules: 12 labours. Celestial sphere: the constellations are back to front.

© I-Spy Limited 1991

ISBN (paperback) 1 85671 011 4
ISBN (hard cover) 1 85671 012 2
Book Club edition CN1979

Michelin Tyre Public Limited Company
Davy House, Lyon Road, Harrow, Middlesex HA1 2DQ

MICHELIN and the Michelin Man are Registered Trademarks of Michelin

A CIP record for this title is available from the British Library.

Edited and designed by Curtis Garratt Limited, The Old Vicarage, Horton cum Studley, Oxford OX9 1BT

The Publisher gratefully acknowledges the contributions of: Storm Dunlop for all text; Wil Tirion for the sky charts and diagrams; Jennifer Garratt for constellation drawings; photographs by Dr Luigi Baldinelli, Denis Buczynski, Storm Dunlop, Peter Gill, David Greenwood, Don Miles, Martin Mobberley, Museum for the History of Science Oxford, Peka Parviainen, Richard Pearce, Regents — University of California, Royal Observatory Greenwich, Royal Observatory Edinburgh.

Colour reproduction by Norwich Litho Services Limited.

Printed in Spain.